The Collector's Series / Volume 31

Just Desserts

by Karla Seidita

AMERICAN
★ COOKING ★
GUILD

Dedication
These recipes are dedicated to all of you who love good eating better than you love good cooking. Good cooking is not necessarily better than good eating. It's just that we believe there are millions of cookbooks already on the market to help you cook very well. That's why we are dedicating this little volume and simple recipes to all you folks who love to eat better than you love to cook.

Acknowledgments
—Edited by Marian Levine
—Illustrations by Debra Trask
—Cover photo courtesy of Karla's Great Cheesecakes, Fredericksburg, Va.

On the cover: Cappuccino Cheesecake, page 15. For the photo, a garnish of whipped cream, rolled cookies and cinnamon have been added.

ISBN 0-942320-38-7

Table of Contents

Cheesecakes

Favorite Pies & Puddings

Cakes, Breads & Other Specialties

Introduction

We've finally grown up as Americans—grown up to American desserts. We're not embarrassed anymore by those cravings that only real American desserts can satisfy. We love to go to church socials and holiday bazaars where ladies decked out in their fanciest white aprons serve up coconut layer cake, fudge ripple brownies or chocolate cream pie. We like our desserts served in large portions—even though our conscience makes us protest at first.

We now know that to be sophisticated and city-wise, you don't have to eat tortes and tarts. Sure, we study them in fancy shop windows. We read about them in fancy food magazines. We even collect more fancy recipes and cookbooks than we care to tell about. But when the chips are down, what we actually crave are American cakes and pies and cookies, along with a heavy dose of brownies and cheesecake.

Secretly, we've always thought all those fancy little tarts and fragile cakes with their foreign sounding names were pretty to look at, but really didn't have much flavor. To this day, my husband has never looked up from his Sunday paper to beg me to whip up a batch of Barquettes aux Marrons.

A while back, a nice young French fellow came to see us. He wanted to open an American bakery back home in Paris. He wanted to know about brownies, cookies, pies and chocolate cake. Most of all, he wanted to know about cheesecake. I knew he had come to the right place. We showed him around, let him taste all the baked goods we could find and talked a lot of technical stuff with him. We were really proud. Can you imagine, American desserts at cafés in Paris?

About Karla's Great Cheesecakes

Karla Seidita is one of a growing number of people who own and operate small food businesses aimed at producing delicious homemade products. Karla's background as a former restaurant owner and home economics educator are put to excellent use in her cottage industry, **Karla's Great Cheesecakes.**

Karla's Great Cheesecakes began in 1985 as a small stand at the Old Town Farmers' Market in Alexandria, Virginia. Starting with half a dozen cheesecakes, Karla has expanded her business over the years to include gooey brownies, fragrant soda breads and lovely cheesecake truffles.

Karla bakes her delicious desserts at Cheesecake Farms in Fredericksburg, Virginia. She calls Cheesecake Farms a state of mind. "It is a place where the water runs pure and the people still smile as they greet you with a hearty hello. It's a place where the tastes and smells of home permeate the air. It's a place where quality and hand work are still prized."

Karla says, "People have always asked me for recipes. I used to tell them to take a pinch of this and a handful of that and bake until done... but it seemed that wasn't enough for some folks!"

Karla's Great Cheesecakes is also a mail order source for spring form pans, cheesecake pans, bulk chocolate, nuts, vanilla, candy cups and other fancy things at farm prices. They can ship selected gifts and baked goods fresh from their bake shop to your family, friends or business associates. Call or write for a product list:

Karla's Great Cheesecakes
Cheesecake Farms
P.O. Box 8451
Fredericksburg, VA 22404
(703) 371-3754

A Word About Ingredients

Cousin Joan came by one day. She is a very smart and educated woman. "These recipes look great, but how did you measure the flour? What about the eggs—are they large, extra large or what?" At that moment, I realized if Cousin Joan wondered about these things, then surely everyone else would. I took it for granted that everyone in the whole world had the benefit of Miss Porter as their 7th grade Home Economics teacher. In case you were not a student of Miss Porter, here are what I call my notes from the stove and afterthoughts from the sink:

Brown sugar: Measure by packing into a measuring cup that will allow you to level off the top. The key is to pack the sugar in. You've packed it properly when you tap it out and it holds the shape of the cup you've measured it in.

Butter: For best results when baking, use butter and not margarine. Margarine leaves you with a slightly more oily finished product. Margarine can be substituted for butter when used in a recipe where there are lots of other ingredients to mask any excess oiliness, such as in a cake. Strudel would not be a good place to use margarine.

Eggs: Use large eggs and take them out of the refrigerator to warm at room temperature for 30 minutes before using. Crack each egg into a small bowl to make sure it is fresh before adding to your recipe.

Cream cheese: Use any brand you like, but avoid whipped, low-fat or diet cream cheese. Leave cream cheese at room temperature overnight to soften. Some people soften cream cheese in the oven or microwave, but you are likely to cook the outside of the cheese before the center is warm.

Flour: Use any brand of regular, all-purpose flour (not self-rising). It can be bleached or unbleached.

Phyllo dough: This paper-thin dough comes in large sheets, packed about 100 sheets to the box. You'll find phyllo dough in the frozen foods section of the grocery store, or in Greek or Middle Eastern stores. Phyllo dough is versatile for strudels, pastries, egg rolls, etc. When you brush phyllo with butter and bake it, it becomes buttery and flaky. To use phyllo, first thaw the dough. Then slice off only the portion you need for your recipe by cutting through the plastic inner wrap with a heavy serrated knife. Refreeze the unused dough (you can thaw and refreeze several times).

Grated lemon, orange or lime peel: Using a grater, scrape off the outer peel of the fruit. Try not to get any of the white part of the peel—it is bitter. Use a fine grater. I sometimes use a vegetable peeler to cut strips of peel and then chop it in a blender.

Vanilla or chocolate cake crumbs: Some recipes in this book call for either vanilla or chocolate cake crumbs. See page 64 for recipes.

Confectionery coating: This is a coating mixture that resembles chocolate in appearance and taste but is easier to work with than chocolate. It does not require tempering but can simply be melted and used.

White chocolate: White chocolate varies in the amount of cocoa butter it contains, from none to a very high amount. White chocolate is much more temperature sensitive than dark chocolate. Melt it at lower temperatures. Once melted, it will thicken again if heating continues.

Cake pan: A pan of lightweight metal with sides about 1 to 2 inches tall. Cake pans come in even sizes like 8 inches, 10 inches or 12 inches in diameter.

Bundt pan: A heavyweight pan with a tube in the middle and rippled sides.

Cheesecake pan: A pan made of heavy metal in odd sizes like 5, 7 or 9 inches. Smaller in diameter and taller in height than cake pans, they allow the cheesecake to bake gently for a longer period of time. Does not have a removable bottom.

Spring form pan: A pan with a hinge on the side and a removable bottom. This kind of pan is used when the batter is thick enough that it won't run out of the joints, but the finished product is so delicate that it can't be removed by inverting the pan. Don't use a spring form pan in a water bath.

Turks Head mold: A tube pan with a swirl design that makes a patterned cake (the kind best served with powdered sugar). It is said to have been invented in Austria after the attempted Ottoman invasion many centuries ago. It was given its name because the shape and swirled effect resembled the hats the Turks wore.

Jelly roll pan: A pan that resembles a cookie sheet, except that it has sides that are 1 inch high. Most jelly roll pans measure 10 x 15 x 1 inches in height.

Baking Tips From A Professional

How to Grease A Pan
All pans that call for greasing should be greased with solid vegetable shortening unless otherwise noted. Use your fingers or a bit of waxed paper to spread shortening around the sides and bottom of the pan, paying attention to corners and edges. Grease to within 1/2 inch from top edge of pan. With Turks Head or Bundt pans, be sure to also grease the center tube. Don't use butter, margarine, oil or a pan spray unless specified.

Measuring Liquids
Liquids are best measured in glass cups that are marked in graduated amounts on the sides. When you think you have poured enough of a liquid ingredient into your measuring cup, hold it at eye level to be sure.

Ways to Melt Chocolate
Use one of the following methods: put chocolate in top pan of a double boiler. Make sure the water in the lower pan is just simmering so there is no steam being produced. Stir occasionally as chocolate melts. Or, put chocolate in a pan and place in an oven set to 200°. Or, melt chocolate in a heavy-bottomed sauce pan over very low heat, stirring constantly.

Preheating The Oven
First, make sure the oven rack is in the center of the oven (unless otherwise specified). Preheat the oven before you begin. For glass or ceramic pans, reduce temperature by 25° and check for doneness 5 minutes earlier.

Testing for Doneness
Cakes are done when the center of the cake is puffed and soft, yet firm to the touch and nicely browned. The sides should be slightly pulled away from the edge of the pan and a toothpick inserted into the center of the cake should be dry when removed. Pies and tarts are done when the crusts are browned, when the juices start to bubble and when a knife stuck into a piece of fruit shows that it's tender. **Cheesecakes baked in a water bath** are done when the top is puffed, the center has risen slightly higher than the rest of the top, and it springs back slightly when touched with the finger. **Cheesecakes baked in a spring form pan** are done when the edges have firmed up about an inch from sides of pan. The center should still be soft. **Cheesecakes baked dry in a cheesecake pan** can vary, so check the recipe for specific instructions.

Removing Cakes From Pans

For some people, removing cakes from the baking pan is a nightmare. For others, it is (excuse the expression) a piece of cake. All recipes in this book should cool for 10 minutes after removing from the oven (unless otherwise stated). Before removing from pan, cut around the perimeter of the pan using a thin, dull knife. Invert the cake onto a flat pan or cooling rack. The cake should slip out of the pan. If not, give the inverted pan a gentle tap on the side or bottom with your hand. (If the cake still doesn't come out, leave the cake inverted in its' pan for several minutes and try again. Some of the trapped steam should help the cake release.) Once the cake has released, invert it again onto a cooling rack to complete cooling.

For a Turks Head or Bundt pan, remove the pan from the oven and cool five minutes. Invert onto a cooling rack, leaving the pan in place. Cool for another five minutes, then lift the pan off the cake. If the pan doesn't lift off easily, reinvert the cake and run a dull knife down between cake and pan wherever it seems to be sticking. Invert again.

Custard-type cheesecakes (those baked in a water bath) should be removed from the water bath and then cooled about 1½ hours at room temperature. Once cool, you can run a long, thin, wet knife around the sides of the pan. Use one smooth motion rather than a sawing motion. Place a piece of plastic wrap on top of the cheesecake. Place a flat dish or pan on top of the plastic wrap (the bottom of a spring form pan works perfectly). Invert the cheesecake onto the flat pan and place on counter. Lightly remove the cheesecake pan. Quickly invert the cake again, this time onto your serving dish. Be careful not to put too much pressure on the cake. Leaving plastic wrap in place, refrigerate overnight.

Let a mousse type cheesecake cool at room temperature for 30 minutes. Then, lightly cover with plastic wrap and refrigerate overnight. The next day, remove the plastic wrap and cut around the cheesecake using a long thin wet knife. Replace the plastic wrap and invert onto a flat pan. Holding the flat pan and the cheesecake.pan, tap several times on the counter to loosen. Invert cake again, this time onto your serving dish.

For cheesecakes baked in a spring form pan, cool 30 minutes, cover with plastic wrap and refrigerate overnight. The next day, run a long thin wet knife around the sides of the pan. Carefully loosen hinge of the pan and remove the side. Leave the cheesecake on the bottom of the pan and place on your serving dish. Nothing could be more simple—except eating out.

More About Cheesecakes

Cutting and Serving

Cheesecakes are, by nature, soft and creamy and they will always stick to a knife. In general, I like to slice my cheesecakes when they are cold, using a piece of waxed or unwaxed dental floss. Stretch the floss across the top of the cake and pull it down. Let go of one end and pull it out from the side at the bottom. A damp, thin knife works well, too. For neater slices, clean the knife between each slice. For taller and lighter cheesecakes (any of the custard types) simply slice thinly and place cut side down on the serving plate. For lower and denser cheesecakes, serve them in small triangles, crust side down. Garnish before or after slices are cut. I prefer fresh fruit, hot or cold fruit compotes, fruit purees, grated chocolate, chopped nuts, cookies or whipped cream. A nice touch is to dust the top of your slices with powdered sugar.

Types of Cheesecakes

Custard Type: A cheesecake usually made with more eggs and no sour cream. Custard type cheesecakes are baked in a water bath for a long, slow baking which develops the custard flavor. These are usually smaller in diameter but taller in height than a New York style cheesecake. Custard type cheesecakes are stable enough to unmold.

New York Style Cheesecake: A cheesecake baked in a spring form pan and made with sour cream. It generally has less eggs than a custard type cheesecake, but since it is baked in a spring form pan, the eggs are not really needed to form a firm structure to allow for unmolding. It is softer, slightly more tart in flavor, usually with a graham cracker crust.

Mousse Type Cheesecake: A soft cheesecake baked dry in a cheesecake pan that is refrigerated overnight before unmolding. The texture is more pudding like than New York style cheesecake and not as firm as a custard type.

How to Bake A Cheesecake in a Water Bath

Fancy cookbooks will call this a Bain Marie. For the water bath use a pan at least 1 inch larger in diameter than your baking pan. First, make your cheesecake and put batter into the smaller pan. Put the filled smaller pan into the empty larger pan. Now fill the larger pan with hot tap water. Place both pans as one unit into the oven. Bake as directed. Remove cheesecake from water bath at the conclusion of baking time. Discard water. Let cheesecake cool on rack until ready to unmold.

Cheesecakes

Karla's Great Cinnamon & Walnut Cheesecake

People are always asking me for a cheesecake recipe and this is one of my favorites. I've always made cheesecakes; in fact, my mother recently sent me an old newspaper article showing me winning a blue ribbon for my cheesecake while I was still in high school. The cheesecake was memorable, of course, but I'd rather forget the photograph.

Yield: one 9-inch spring form pan; 12-16 servings.

Crust:
- *1/2 cup melted butter or margarine*
- *1 1/2 cups graham cracker crumbs*
- *1/2 teaspoon cinnamon*
- *1 1/2 cup walnuts, coarsely chopped*

Filling:
- *1 pound cream cheese, softened*
- *1 cup sugar*
- *2 teaspoons vanilla*
- *3 eggs*
- *3 cups sour cream*

Preheat oven to 375°. In a medium size bowl, mix together all crust ingredients and then press into the bottom of a 9-inch spring form pan. Set aside.

In a large bowl, place cream cheese, sugar and vanilla and beat with an electric mixer until very smooth and fluffy. Beat in eggs, one at a time. Add sour cream and mix until just combined. Pour into prepared crust and bake for 35 minutes at 375°. Cheesecake should be set but center will not be firm. Chill overnight before cutting.

Peanut Butter and Jelly Cheesecake

A childhood staple with grown-up style.

Yield: one 7-inch round cheesecake, 8-12 servings.

$^1/_2$ *cup vanilla pound cake crumbs (page 64)*
$1^1/_2$ *pounds cream cheese, softened*
1 *cup sugar*
1 *Tablespoon cornstarch*
$^3/_4$ *teaspoon vanilla*
4 *eggs*
$^1/_2$ *recipe for Peanut Butter Brownies (page 48), baked*
$^3/_4$ *cup tart jelly or jam (red raspberry or currant)*
  at room temperature or slightly warmed
$^3/_4$ *cup salted peanuts, chopped*

Preheat oven to 325°. Grease bottom and sides of a 7-inch cheesecake pan. Sprinkle cake crumbs evenly over bottom of pan.

In a large bowl, using an electric mixer, beat together cream cheese, sugar, cornstarch and vanilla until cheese mixture is soft and fluffy. Add eggs and mix until just combined. Pour half of mixture into prepared pan. Coarsely crumble peanut butter brownies over top. Pour remaining batter over crumbs. Bake in a water bath for 50-60 minutes at 325° or until top is nicely browned and center is slightly puffed.

Remove from water bath and cool at room temperature at least 1½ hours. Invert cake onto serving dish. Refrigerate overnight. Before serving, spread jelly over top and garnish edge of cake with chopped nuts.

Cappuccino Cheesecake

We've been making this cheesecake for a lovely little Italian restaurant in Washington, D.C. for many years. They think it goes particularly well after their Italian dinners. We agree.

Yield: one 9-inch spring form pan, 12-16 servings.

> 1¹/₂ *cups chocolate cake crumbs (page 64)*
> 1¹/₂ *pounds cream cheese, softened*
> 1¹/₂ *cups sugar*
>   1 *Tablespoon ground espresso or French Roast coffee (dry coffee)*
>   2 *teaspoons vanilla*
>   3 *eggs*
> 1¹/₂ *pints sour cream*

Preheat oven to 375°. Sprinkle cake crumbs over the bottom of an ungreased 9-inch spring form pan. Distribute the crumbs evenly and press down lightly. Set aside while preparing cheesecake batter.

In a large bowl, using an electric mixer, beat together cream cheese, sugar, dry coffee and vanilla until smooth and fluffy (about five minutes). Add eggs, one at a time, mixing just to incorporate. Add sour cream all at once and blend well. Pour into prepared pan and bake at 375° for 35-40 minutes. Cheesecake will appear set but not done. Remove from oven, cool, wrap in plastic wrap and refrigerate overnight.

Before serving, remove sides of pan (See Removing Cakes From Pans on page 10). Serve with a dollop of freshly whipped cream and a pinch of cinnamon or grated chocolate.

Milk Chocolate Amaretto Mousse Cheesecake

At Cheesecake Farms, we like to serve this with Amaretto-laced coffee. It is delicious with a dollop of freshly whipped cream.

Yield: one 7-inch cheesecake, 8-12 servings.

- ¹/₂ cup vanilla pound cake crumbs
- 1 ounce unsweetened chocolate, melted
- 1¹/₂ pounds cream cheese, softened
- 1¹/₂ cups sugar
- 2 teaspoons cornstarch
- 1 Tablespoon Amaretto liqueur
- 2 teaspoons almond extract
- 2 teaspoons ground espresso or French roast coffee (dry coffee)
- ¹/₂ teaspoon vanilla
- 1 egg

Preheat oven to 350°. Grease the bottom of a 7-inch cheesecake pan. Sprinkle the pound cake crumbs over the bottom of the pan. Set aside while preparing cheesecake batter.

In a large bowl, using an electric mixer, beat together chocolate, cream cheese, sugar, cornstarch, Amaretto liqueur, almond extract, dry coffee and vanilla until smooth and fluffy (about five minutes). Scrape bowl frequently, incorporating all ingredients. Add egg and mix just to combine. Pour over prepared crust. Bake at 350° for 25-30 minutes. Cheesecake will be puffed and set, but not firm. Remove from oven, cool, cover with plastic wrap and refrigerate overnight.

Before serving, run knife around inside of pan and unmold. (Refer to Removing Cakes From Pans on page 10.)

Chocolate Chip and Walnut Cheesecake

If you love both chocolate chip cookies and cheesecake, this one is for you.

Yield: one 9-inch spring form pan, 12-16 servings.

1¹/2   cups chocolate cake crumbs (page 64)
1   pound cream cheese, softened
1   cup sugar
1   teaspoon vanilla
3   eggs
2   cups sour cream
¹/2   cup walnuts, coarsely chopped
¹/2   cup semi-sweet chocolate chips

Preheat oven to 375°. Evenly sprinkle cake crumbs over the bottom of a 9-inch spring form pan. Press crumbs down lightly.

In a large bowl, using an electric mixer, beat together cream cheese, sugar and vanilla until smooth and fluffy. Stir in eggs and sour cream. Fold in walnuts and chocolate chips. Pour into prepared pan. Bake at 375° for 35 minutes. Remove from oven and refrigerate overnight before cutting.

Serve with a dollop of freshly whipped cream and a drizzle of chocolate syrup.

Variations:
Mint Chocolate Chip Cheesecake: Substitute mint chocolate chips for the semi-sweet chocolate chips and omit the walnuts.

Lemon Chocolate Chip Cheesecake: Omit walnuts and add the grated rind of one lemon.

Palm Beach Fresh Orange Cheesecake

The fresh orange taste will remind you of sunny Florida.

Yield: one 7-inch round cheesecake, 8-12 servings.

> *$^1/_2$ cup vanilla pound cake crumbs (page 64)*
> *$1^1/_2$ pounds cream cheese, softened*
> *1   cup sugar*
> *1   Tablespoon cornstarch*
> *$^3/_4$ teaspoon vanilla*
> *1   Tablespoon fresh orange rind, grated*
> *4   eggs*

Preheat oven to 325°. Grease the bottom and sides of a 7-inch cheesecake pan. Sprinkle crumbs evenly over bottom.

In a large bowl, using an electric mixer, beat together cream cheese, sugar, cornstarch, vanilla and orange rind until soft and fluffy. Add eggs and mix until just combined. Pour into crust.

Bake in a water bath at 325° for about 50-60 minutes or until top is browned and center is slightly puffed. Remove from water bath. Cool at room temperature at least 1½ hours before unmolding. Invert onto a flat pan and invert again onto serving dish. Refrigerate overnight before cutting.

Variation: Substitute lemon rind for orange rind.

Light Lemonade Cheesecake

This is a light cheesecake because it is made with cottage cheese instead of cream cheese and just the white of the egg is used instead of the whole egg. It is easily made in a blender or food processor.

Yield: one 7-inch round cheesecake, 8-12 servings.

3	egg whites
	rind of half a lemon
1/8	teaspoon vanilla
2/3	cup sugar
1/4	cup cornstarch
2²/3	cups cottage cheese

Preheat oven to 325°. Grease the bottom of a 7-inch cheesecake pan.

Place all ingredients in a blender or processor. Blend until smooth. Pour into pan.

Bake in a water bath at 325° for approximately 70 minutes, until center is set and toothpick comes out clean. Remove from water bath and refrigerate overnight.

Before serving, remove cake from pan by cutting around edges and inverting onto flat pan. Invert again onto a serving dish. Serve with fresh fruit, such as peaches or crushed pineapple.

Cheesecake Flan

This make-ahead dessert is fast and easy, and is especially good after Mexican or Spanish meals.

Yield: one 7-inch round flan, 8-12 servings.

> *1/2*   *cup water*
> *1/2*   *cup sugar*
> *1*   *pound cream cheese, softened*
> *5*   *eggs*
> *1*   *14 ounce can sweetened condensed milk*
> *1*   *12 ounce can evaporated milk*

Preheat oven to 350°. In a small heavy frying pan, melt water and sugar together and bring to a boil. Continue boiling until syrup is golden brown. Once the syrup turns brown, it will continue to darken and may burn— watch the pan continuously and work quickly. Immediately pour all the syrup into the bottom of a 7-inch cheesecake pan and rotate pan to cover bottom. Syrup will harden quickly, so work fast. Set aside.

In a large bowl, using an electric mixer, beat cream cheese until smooth. Beat in eggs, one at a time. Slowly beat in condensed milk. Stir in evaporated milk. Pour into prepared pan. Bake in a water bath at 350° for 70-75 minutes or until a toothpick inserted in the center comes out clean. Cool, then refrigerate overnight.

To unmold, cut around sides of pan with a knife. Dip the bottom of the pan into one inch of hot water and hold for two minutes. Invert onto a flat serving dish with a rim to catch the syrup. Unmold, shaking the pan a bit to get a little air down to the bottom (gravity will pull the flan out). Serve as is or with a dollop of freshly whipped cream. The hardened caramelized sugar makes a light liquid caramel sauce.

Lemon and Black Walnut Cheesecake

We have lots of black walnut trees at Cheesecake Farms. Some years we get a nice big crop of nuts. Other years the squirrels get them. Don't substitute any other nuts for the black walnuts—it just isn't the same.

Yield: one 9-inch spring form pan, 12-16 servings.

Cheesecake:
- 1¹/₂ *cups vanilla pound cake crumbs (page 64)*
- 1 *pound cream cheese, softened*
- 1 *cup sugar*
- 1¹/₂ *teaspoons vanilla*
- 3 *eggs*
- 2 *cups sour cream*
- 1 *recipe Lemon Curd (recipe below)*
- ³/₄ *cup black walnuts, coarsely chopped*

Lemon Curd:
- 3 *Tablespoons cornstarch*
- ¹/₂ *cup sugar*
- ¹/₂ *cup lemon juice*
- ¹/₄ *cup butter*
- 3 *eggs*

Cheesecake:
Preheat oven to 375°. Evenly sprinkle pound cake crumbs over bottom of a 9-inch spring form pan. Press crumbs down lightly. In a large bowl, using an electric mixer, beat together cream cheese, sugar and vanilla until smooth and fluffy. Stir in eggs and sour cream. Pour over prepared crust. Bake for 35 minutes at 375° or until just set. Refrigerate overnight before cutting.

Lemon Curd:
In a small heavy saucepan mix together cornstarch and sugar. Add lemon juice and butter. Heat, whisking constantly until thick. In a medium bowl, whisk eggs together until well mixed. Add a small bit of the hot mixture, whisking constantly. Gradually add the remaining hot mixture until all is incorporated. Do not add all at once or the result will be scrambled eggs!

To serve: Top cheesecake with cooled Lemon Curd and decorate edge with black walnuts.

Cup Custard Cheesecake

We call this Cup Custard Cheesecake because the long, slow baking really develops the old-timey cup custard flavor. Nice served plain or with any fresh fruit in season. In the winter, top this with a hot winter fruit compote. Or, microwave slices of cake and serve warm.

Yield: one 7-inch round cheesecake, 8-12 servings.

$1/2$	cup vanilla pound cake crumbs (page 64)
$1^1/2$	pounds cream cheese, softened
1	cup sugar
1	Tablespoon cornstarch
$1/2$	teaspoon vanilla
4	eggs

Preheat oven to 325°. Grease the bottom and sides of a 7-inch cheesecake pan. Sprinkle crumbs evenly over bottom.

In a large bowl, using an electric mixer, beat together cream cheese, sugar, cornstarch and vanilla until soft and fluffy. Add eggs and mix until just combined.

Pour into prepared pan and bake in a water bath at 325° for 50-60 minutes or until top is nicely browned and center is slightly puffed. Remove from water bath. Cool at room temperature at least $1\frac{1}{2}$ hours before unmolding. To unmold, invert onto a flat pan and invert again onto serving dish. Refrigerate overnight before cutting.

Tropical Coconut and Lime Cheesecake

This is fabulous for the summertime. You don't bake this cheesecake so you can have a yummy dessert without a hot kitchen. Wonderfully light and fluffy, and always a bit hit.

Yield: one 9-inch spring form pan, 12-16 servings.

Crust:
      1   Tablespoon butter
    1½   cups vanilla pound cake crumbs (page 64)
      1   cup coconut

Filling:
      1   envelope unflavored gelatin
      1   cup water, divided
      3   eggs, separated
      1   cup sugar
      1   cup heavy cream
      1   pound cream cheese
      2   teaspoons grated lime peel (1 large lime)
    ¼   cup lime juice

Use the tablespoon of butter to generously grease the bottom of a 9-inch spring form pan. Press cake crumbs over bottom. Sprinkle coconut over crumbs. Set aside.

Stir unflavored gelatin into ¼ cup water to soften. In a small heavy saucepan, whisk together softened gelatin, egg yolks, ¾ cup water and sugar. Heat, whisking constantly until mixture is steaming. Do not boil. Pour into a bowl and refrigerate for five minutes.

Meanwhile, in a large bowl, beat egg whites until stiff. In another bowl, beat heavy cream until stiff. In a third bowl, beat cream cheese until very smooth. Add lime juice and rind to cream cheese. Fold everything together including the refrigerated mixture. Pour over prepared crust and refrigerate overnight. Garnish with additional whipped cream if desired.

Variation:
Use lemon or orange rind and juice instead of lime. Hint: the juice of one lemon or lime probably will not make 1/4 cup so be prepared with some bottled juice.

Princeton Cheesecake

Bittersweet chocolate and orange liqueur makes this the richest cheesecake ever. Garnish each piece with a dollop of freshly whipped cream and an orange slice. One slice and you'll purr like a tiger.

Yield: one 9-inch spring form pan, 12-16 servings.

> 1½ cups chocolate cake crumbs (page 64)
> 12 ounces cream cheese, softened
> 2 cups sugar
> 1½ teaspoons vanilla
> 6 squares (6 ounces) unsweetened chocolate
> 1 egg
> 1 cup sour cream
> 6 Tablespoons orange liqueur

Preheat oven to 350°. Evenly distribute crumbs over bottom of a 9-inch spring form pan. Press crumbs down lightly.

In a medium bowl, using an electric mixer, beat together cream cheese, sugar and vanilla until smooth and fluffy. Set aside.

In a small, heavy saucepan, melt chocolate over low heat. Stir constantly. Pour melted chocolate all at once into cheese mixture and beat until combined. Add egg and beat until very smooth, about five minutes. Add sour cream and liqueur and mix until combined. Pour batter over prepared crust.

Bake at 350° for 25-30 minutes or until just set. Refrigerate overnight before serving.

Virginia Peanut Butter Creme Cheesecake

This recipe is especially for those who must have their peanut butter smooth and throughout their cheesecake. Serve with hot, melted red raspberry or currant jelly, or with bittersweet hot fudge sauce drizzled over the top.

Yield: one 7-inch round cheesecake, 8-12 servings.

1/2	*cup vanilla pound cake crumbs (page 64)*
12	*ounces cream cheese, softened*
3/4	*cup sugar*
1/2	*cup creamy peanut butter (commercial type, not freshly ground)*
1	*teaspoon salt*
4	*eggs*
3/4	*teaspoon vanilla*

Preheat oven to 350°. Grease the bottom of a 7-inch round cheesecake pan. Distribute crumbs over bottom. Set aside.

In a large bowl, using an electric mixer, beat cream cheese and sugar together. When smooth and fluffy, add peanut butter and salt and beat well. Mix in eggs, one at a time. Stir in vanilla. Pour into prepared pan.

Bake in a water bath at 350° for 50-60 minutes. Remove from oven and cool at room temperature at least 90 minutes before unmolding. To unmold, invert onto a flat pan and invert again onto serving dish. Refrigerate overnight before cutting.

Turn Off The Oven Cheesecake

Some folks don't believe that a cheesecake can be done when it doesn't look dry and firm. This recipe is especially for beginning bakers who don't quite trust their judgement.

Yield: one 9-inch spring form pan, 12-16 servings.

Crust:
>   2   *Tablespoons sugar*
>   2   *Tablespoons melted butter*
> 1½   *cups graham cracker crumbs*

Filling:
>   1   *pound cream cheese, softened*
>   1   *cup sugar*
>   1   *teaspoon vanilla*
>   3   *eggs*
>   2   *cups sour cream*

Preheat oven to 375°.

In a small bowl combine sugar, butter and graham cracker crumbs. Use a fork or your fingers to mix ingredients together and sprinkle evenly over the bottom of a 9-inch spring form pan. Set aside.

In a medium bowl put cream cheese, sugar and vanilla. Beat with an electric mixer until mixture is fluffy and free of lumps. Add eggs, one at a time, mixing until they just combine. Add sour cream and mix until smooth.

Pour batter into prepared crust and bake at 375° for 30 minutes. Without opening oven door, turn off the heat and leave cheesecake in oven for one hour more. Remove from oven and refrigerate overnight. Remove from spring form pan before serving.

Creamsickle Cheesecake

This is an adult version of a childhood favorite ice cream bar. Equally good, we feel.

Yield: one 9-inch spring form pan, 12-16 servings.

1¹/₂	*cups vanilla pound cake crumbs (page 64)*
1	*pound cream cheese, softened*
1	*cup sugar*
1¹/₂	*teaspoons vanilla*
¹/₄	*cup orange liqueur*
3	*eggs*
2	*cups sour cream*

Preheat oven to 375°. Evenly sprinkle the pound cake crumbs over the bottom of an ungreased spring form pan. Press crumbs down lightly.

Using an electric mixer, in a large bowl, cream together cream cheese, sugar, vanilla and orange liqueur until mixture is smooth. Stir in eggs and sour cream. Pour batter over prepared crust. Bake at 375° for 35 minutes.

Remove from oven and refrigerate overnight before serving. Serve with a dollop of freshly whipped cream.

Cheesecake Framboise

Milk chocolate and raspberry brandy combine for an elegant, rich and creamy cheesecake. Serve with freshly whipped cream and a sprinkle of powdered sugar.

Yield: one 9-inch spring form pan, 12-16 servings.

> 1¹/₂   cups vanilla pound cake crumbs (page 64)
> ¹/₄   cup Half and Half cream (or evaporated milk)
> 6   ounces semi-sweet chocolate chips
> 1¹/₂   pounds cream cheese, softened
> 1   cup sugar
> 1   teaspoon vanilla
> ¹/₄   cup Framboise
> ¹/₄   cup brewed, cold espresso or French roast coffee
> 2   eggs
> 1   cup sour cream

Preheat oven to 350°. Distribute pound cake crumbs evenly over the bottom of a 9-inch spring form pan and lightly press down. Set crust aside while making cheesecake batter.

In a small heavy saucepan, melt together the Half and Half or evaporated milk and chocolate chips. Stir over low heat until smooth and well combined. Remove from heat.

Using an electric mixer, in a large bowl, beat together cream cheese, sugar and vanilla until light and fluffy, about five minutes. Add Framboise, coffee and eggs, mixing well. Add chocolate and mix again. Mixture should be very smooth at this point. Add sour cream and mix again until just combined.

Pour into prepared crust and bake at 350° for approximately 45 minutes. Cheesecake will be slightly puffed and set about 1 inch around pan, and center will be semi-set. Remove from oven and cool. Cover and refrigerate overnight. Before serving, cut around sides of pan and remove hinged sides (see Removing Cakes From Pans on page 10).

Note: This cake can be made in a food processor. Combine the batter ingredients all at once and blend until smooth. Be sure your processor container is large enough to accommodate all ingredients.

Pistachio Cheesecake

A simple cake with no baking involved—the perfect recipe for those occasions when you have to bring a dessert but don't have time to make one!

Yield: one 9-inch spring form pan, 12-16 servings

> 1   *Tablespoon butter*
> 1¹/₂ *cups vanilla pound cake crumbs (page 64)*
> 5¹/₂ *cups sour cream, at room temperature*
> 2   *3 ³/₄ ounce packages pistachio instant pudding mix*
> 3   *Tablespoons almond extract*

Grease the bottom of a 9-inch spring form pan with the butter. Distribute the pound cake crumbs over the greased bottom of the pan, pressing down lightly. Set aside while preparing filling.

In a large bowl, using an electric mixer, beat together sour cream, pudding mix and almond extract. Pour into crumb lined pan. Lightly cover and chill overnight in the refrigerator. To serve, cut around the sides of the pan with a wet knife. Loosen hinge and remove sides of pan. Garnish lavishly with whipped cream.

Note: The pudding mix is used in the dry form. The sour cream substitutes for the mix.

Aunt Anna's Honey, Raisin & Nut Cheesecake

During the Second World War, Aunt Anna often helped folks out with lodgings and letter writing. One day, a lady that Aunt Anna had helped quite a bit gave her this recipe as a small thank you. She had brought it from somewhere in Eastern Europe and said it was served for Easter breakfast or Christmas Eve. We've enjoyed it ever since.

Yield: one 8-inch square pan, 16 servings

Crust:
1	cup flour
1/4	cup sugar
1/4	teaspoon salt
4	Tablespoons butter
1	egg

Filling:
1/4	cup dark raisins
1/4	cup walnuts
3	cups cottage cheese
4	eggs
1/2	cup honey
1/4	cup flour
1/4	cup sugar
	rind of one lemon, grated
1/2	teaspoon vanilla
1/4	teaspoon salt
1/8	teaspoon cinnamon

Preheat oven to 350°. In a medium bowl, mix crust ingredients together with a fork or fingers, forming dough into a ball. Press dough into the bottom and halfway up the sides of an ungreased 8-inch square pan.

Sprinkle the raisins and walnuts over crust in the pan. In a large bowl, stir together remaining ingredients except the cinnamon. Pour batter over the raisins and nuts and sprinkle cinnamon over top. Bake at 350° for about 40 minutes or until center of the cake is set but not brown. Cool before cutting into small squares. Serve cold or at room temperature.

Cheesecake Easter Egg

Can you imagine cutting into a lavishly decorated Easter egg to find that it is actually a creamy cheesecake? If you are skilled, make your own butter cream flowers to decorate the egg. If not, buy pre-made royal icing flowers (write to me if you can't find them in your area).

Yield: one large Easter egg or two small eggs, 8-10 servings

> 1   *baked custard-type cheesecake, any flavor, refrigerated overnight*
> ½   *pound confectionery coating, any color**
>   *vegetable shortening*
>   *assorted pre-made icing flowers or other decorations**
>   *buttercream icing, tinted a pale color*

Using a cold or slightly frozen custard-type cheesecake, mold it into one large or two smaller egg shapes. Lightly dampen hands if necessary (it is much the same as making a meat loaf). Work quickly, handling cheesecake as little as possible. Smooth surface with a dampened spatula. Place onto serving dish and refrigerate or freeze while melting coating.

Melt confectionery coating in top of double boiler. Use a bit of vegetable shortening to thin the coating if it seems too thick—for best results, coating must not be too hot or too thick when spreading onto the egg. Spread coating onto egg in several thin layers, refrigerating to set coating between layers. When last layer has set, decorate the egg with flowers. Use a bit of coating or buttercream icing as glue. Pipe on leaves or other decorations using icing in a pastry bag. Refrigerate overnight before serving.

*You will find confectionery coating and pre-made icing flowers in kitchen and gourmet stores, or in craft stores that also sell cake decorating and candy molding supplies.

Patriotic Cheesecake

An easy and delicious way to celebrate July 4th or other patriotic events.

Yield: one 7-inch cheesecake, 8-10 servings.

> 1 *recipe Cup Custard Cheesecake, baked and*
>   *refrigerated overnight (page 22)*
> 1 *cup blueberry pie filling*
> 1 *cup strawberries or cherry pie filling*
> 1 *container (12 ounces) whipped topping or*
>   *2 cups heavy cream, whipped and sweetened to taste*

Frost the entire cheesecake with whipped topping or cream. Spread blueberry pie filling on one fourth of the cake for the blue background for stars. Arrange strawberries or cherry pie filling in stripes across rest of cake. Using a pastry bag, pipe whipped topping or whipped cream stars onto blueberry filling. Use extra cream to define the white stripes. Refrigerate until serving time.

White Chocolate Cheesecake

My favorite, everybody's favorite—this is our most requested recipe. Don't be fooled—this recipe does not contain eggs. Bake as directed and it will firm up overnight in the refrigerator.

Yield: one 9-inch spring form pan, 12-16 servings.

12	ounces white chocolate
1¹/₄	cups vanilla pound cake crumbs (page 64)
1¹/₂	pounds cream cheese, softened
1	cup sugar
2 ¹/₂	teaspoons vanilla
1	Tablespoon apricot brandy
2	cups sour cream

Melt white chocolate (see Baking Tips on page 9). Preheat oven to 350°. Distribute pound cake crumbs evenly over the bottom of a 9-inch spring form pan. Press crumbs down lightly. Set aside.

In a large bowl, cream together cream cheese, sugar, vanilla and apricot brandy with an electric mixer for at least five minutes or until very smooth. Add melted white chocolate and blend another five minutes. Add sour cream and mix to combine. Pour into crumb lined pan and bake at 350° for 30 minutes. Chill overnight before serving.

Note: To make in a food processor, put all batter ingredients into processor and blend until smooth. Make sure the processor bowl is large enough to hold all ingredients, and that the chocolate is completely melted.

Pies, Puddings
& Fruit Desserts

Peaches and Cream Cobbler

This luscious dessert can be made at the very last minute if some guests pop in. In the summertime, we use fresh peaches and in the winter we use our home canned peaches.

Yield: one 8-inch casserole, 4-6 servings.

Crust:
1	cup flour
1/4	teaspoon baking powder
1/4	teaspoon salt
1	Tablespoon sugar
7	Tablespoons butter

Filling:
4-5	fresh peaches, peeled, pitted and sliced or 1 can (1 lb. 15 oz.) sliced peaches, drained
1/2	teaspoon cinnamon
1/2	cup sugar
2	egg yolks
1	cup sour cream

Preheat oven to 375°. Make crust by working crust ingredients together with a fork or fingers until a soft dough forms. Shape into a ball and press dough into the bottom of an ungreased glass or ceramic casserole dish measuring 8-inches round and 3-inches deep. Top dough with peaches, cinnamon and sugar. Bake at 375° for 20 minutes.

Mix together egg yolks and sour cream. After cobbler has baked 20 minutes, pour sour cream mixture over peaches and bake another 20-25 minutes, until topping is set. To serve, spoon from casserole onto serving plates. Serve hot or cold.

Coconut Fudge Pie

Serve cold with a dollop of freshly whipped cream and a bit of grated orange rind. Or, once the pie has chilled overnight, you can serve it hot by warming single slices in the microwave.

Yield: one 10-inch pie, 12-16 servings

2	Tablespoons butter
3	cups coconut, divided
1	can (13 ounces) evaporated milk
3/4	cup brewed, double strength coffee
8	ounces semi-sweet chocolate chips
1 1/3	cups light brown sugar
2	eggs
6	Tablespoons flour
2	Tablespoons Amaretto, Creme de Cocoa or coffee liqueur

Preheat the oven to 350°. Use the entire 2 tablespoons butter to grease the bottom, sides and rim of a 10-inch pie pan. Press 2 3/4 cups coconut around sides and bottom of pan to form crust. Save 1/4 cup coconut for top edge of pie.

In a small saucepan, melt together evaporated milk, coffee and chocolate chips. Heat to steaming but do not boil. In a large bowl, whisk together brown sugar, eggs and flour. Add hot milk mixture a little at a time, whisking well. Pour into coconut-lined pie shell. Use remaining 1/4 cup coconut to edge the pie at the rim, making a neat edge.

Bake at 350° for about 25 minutes, until just set but not firm. Coconut will be light brown in color. Refrigerate overnight before serving.

Apple and Oat Crisp

If you hate to make crust, try crisp! I like to use yellow Delicious apples in this recipe.

Yield: one 8-inch casserole, 6-10 servings

- $1/2$ cup butter, softened
- 1   cup light brown sugar
- $1/2$ cup flour
- $1/2$ cup oatmeal, uncooked
- 10   apples, pared and coarsely chopped (8 cups)

Preheat oven to 350°. Grease an ovenproof casserole measuring 8 inches round x 3 inches deep. In a medium size bowl, use a fork to combine all ingredients except apples to make a coarse meal. Starting with apples, alternately layer apples and crumbs in casserole, ending with crumbs.

Bake at 350° for 45-60 minutes until apples are soft and crumbs are golden brown. Serve warm with a scoop of vanilla ice cream.

Apricot Strudel

This is an easy strudel made with phyllo dough layered into a square pan. It tastes every bit as good as a rolled strudel, with only a fraction of the work.

Yield: one 8-inch square pan, 8-10 servings.

> 5   cups fresh apricots, pitted and halved but not peeled
>   or 2 cans (30 ounces each) apricot halves in heavy syrup,
>   drained
> $1/2$ cup butter (do not use margarine)
> 5   ounces phyllo dough ($1/3$ of a 15 ounce package)
> $1/2$ cup sugar (use $1/3$ cup for canned apricots)
> 2   Tablespoons instant (or quick cooking) tapioca

Preheat oven to 350°. In a small saucepan, melt the butter. Using a pastry brush, brush butter on sides and bottom of an 8-inch square pan. Put a layer of phyllo dough on bottom. Brush again with butter, then add another layer of phyllo. Repeat process for a total of four layers.

In a large bowl, combine apricots, sugar and tapioca. Spread mixture over buttered dough. Continue layering phyllo and butter until all dough is used. End with butter. Pour any remaining butter over the top.

Bake at 350° for about 25 minutes, or until dough is lightly browned. Best served the same day it is baked. To serve, dust heavily with powdered sugar and serve with a scoop of vanilla ice cream.

Grandma's Old Fashioned Baked Rice Pudding

This is a very old recipe, updated for today's tastes. You can make it with leftover white or brown rice. You can serve it hot, cold, even at room temperature. At Cheesecake Farms, we serve it for breakfast with a bit of hot milk.

Yield: one 9-inch loaf, 4-6 servings

1½	cups cooked rice
½	cup sugar
3	eggs
1	teaspoon vanilla
3	Tablespoons white raisins, plumped in hot water
1	can (12 ounces) evaporated milk
⅛	teaspoon cinnamon

Preheat oven to 325°. Lightly butter a 9"x 5"x 3" loaf pan. In a medium bowl, mix all ingredients except cinnamon. Pour into prepared pan. Sprinkle cinnamon on top. Bake at 325° for 1 hour, or until just set.

Brown Sugar Pear Pie

Use fresh pears if you happen to have a pear tree in your yard. As pies go, you really can't tell the difference between fresh and canned pears once the pie is baked, as you can with other fruits like apples. If you use fresh pears, make sure they are ripe, peeled and cored. You'll need about 15 fresh pears for a 10-inch pie.

Yield: one 10-inch double crust pie, 8-12 servings.

   1   *double pie crust, homemade or store bought*
   3   *cans (30 ounces each) pear halves in heavy syrup, drained*
   1/3 *cup dark brown sugar, or more to taste*
   1   *Tablespoon instant (or quick cooking) tapioca*
   1/4 *cup butter*

Place oven rack in lowest position. Preheat oven to 400°. Line the pie pan with one crust. Toss pears lightly with brown sugar and tapioca. Pour into pie crust. Cut butter into little bits and sprinkle over pears. Top with second crust. Crimp edges and cut a steam hole in center. Bake at 400° for 25 minutes or until crust is browned. If using fresh pears, bake a bit longer until pears are soft when poked with a knife through the steam hole.

Serve hot or cold with a big scoop of vanilla or rum raisin ice cream.

Cranberry and Crisp Apple Pie

When I was in high school, I won a blue ribbon for baking this pie. Besides the ribbon, I got 5 gallons of ice cream—now that was a prize!

Yield: one 10-inch double crust pie, 8-10 servings

    1   double pie crust, homemade or store bought
    1   can (16 ounces) whole cranberry sauce
    1/2 cup sugar
    2   Tablespoons instant (or quick cooking) tapioca
    6   cups green or pie apples (about 10)
    1/3 cup walnuts, chopped

Preheat oven to 400°. Line a 10-inch pie pan with bottom crust. In a large pot, over medium heat, melt cranberry sauce. Remove from heat, add sugar, tapioca and apples. Stir to coat. Pour into crust. Sprinkle with walnuts. Cover with top crust. Flute edges and cut steam vents.

Bake at 400° for about 50 minutes, until crust is nicely browned and apples are tender.

Unsugared Apple Pie

This pie is surprisingly sweet and yet is made without any added sugar. We think it's a thoughtful dessert to serve when you know your guests are restricting their sugar intake. Now mind you, we don't make any particular health claims for this pie, we simply say it's a bit more virtuous.

Yield: one 10-inch pie, 8-12 servings.

1	double pie crust, homemade or store bought
12	large Delicious apples, peeled, cored and coarsely chopped (about 10 cups)
$^1/_4$	cup dark raisins
$^1/_4$	cup walnuts, coarsely chopped
$^3/_4$	cup unsweetened apple juice
1	Tablespoon butter
1	Tablespoon instant (or quick cooking) tapioca
$^1/_4$	teaspoon vanilla

Place oven rack in lowest position. Preheat oven to 400°.

Line pie pan with bottom crust. Fill crust with apples, raisins and walnuts. In a small saucepan, heat juice, butter, tapioca and vanilla until butter melts. Pour over apples. Top with second crust. Crimp edges and cut a steam hold in center of pie.

Bake at 400° for 50 minutes or until crust is browned. Cool before cutting. Virtue may, upon occasion, be compromised by serving this unsugared pie with a scoop of vanilla ice cream.

Plum Crumb Pie

People always think that folks who can bake pies are the best cooks around. You won't tell them how easy this is, will you?

Yield: one 10-inch pie, 8-12 servings.

Crust:
2	cups all-purpose flour
1¼	teaspoons baking powder
4	teaspoons sugar
2	eggs
3	Tablespoons butter or margarine

Filling:
8	cups fresh Italian plums (prune plums) washed, pitted and quartered (do not peel)
⅓	cup light brown sugar, or more to taste
⅛	teaspoon nutmeg
¼	teaspoon cinnamon

Topping:
1	cup all-purpose flour
¾	cup light brown sugar
6	Tablespoons butter

Place oven rack in lowest position. Preheat oven to 350°.

In a medium bowl, using an electric mixer, combine all crust ingredients until dough forms a ball. Press dough into a 10-inch ungreased pie pan. Be careful to keep dough of a uniform thickness, especially where the sides of pan meet the bottom. Flute edges.

Toss all filling ingredients together and place in pastry-lined pie pan.

In a medium bowl, use a fork to lightly toss together all topping ingredients, making a crumbly mixture. Do not mix too long or crumbs will start to blend together. Sprinkle crumbs over top of pie. Bake at 350° for about 30 minutes until crust is browned and fruit begins to get soft and juicy. Serve warm or cold, with ice cream if desired.

Hot Fudge Pudding Cake

This dessert separates as it bakes into a pudding layer on the bottom and a cake layer on the top. Serve hot from the oven, scooping cake and pudding into a bowl. Top with freshly whipped cream and cinnamon, or ice cream. On days that I'm blue, I make a pan of this and grab a spoon as soon as it comes out of the oven. Sometimes I do stop to pour myself a glass of milk.

Yield: one 8-inch square pan, 4-6 servings.

1	cup all-purpose flour
3/4	cup sugar
2	Tablespoons plus 1/4 cup cocoa, divided
2	teaspoons baking powder
1/4	teaspoon salt
1/2	cup milk
2	Tablespoons melted butter
1	cup light brown sugar
1 3/4	cups boiling water

Preheat oven to 350°. In an ungreased 8-inch square pan, mix together flour, sugar, 2 tablespoons cocoa, baking powder and salt. Add milk and butter. Mix well. In a small bowl, mix together brown sugar and remaining cocoa. Sprinkle over dough. Do not stir. Next, pour boiling water over top. Stir twice around and no more! Bake 20-25 minutes until cake is set and pudding is bubbling.

Mile High Strawberry Pie

Want to get the best strawberries around? They're not in the stores. They're at the roadside stands and at the farmers' markets. That's where the fruit has been left on the vines to ripen. You cannot beat a vine-ripened berry.

Yield: one 10-inch pie, 8-12 servings

Crust:

$^3/4$	*cup butter*
$2^1/2$	*cups all-purpose flour*
1	*Tablespoon sugar*
3	*Tablespoons milk*

Filling:

3	*quarts strawberries, washed, hulled and sliced*
1	*cup sugar*
3	*Tablespoons cornstarch*
$^1/2$	*cup water*
1	*Tablespoon lemon juice*

Preheat oven to 425°. In a medium bowl, cut butter into flour and sugar. Add milk. Form into a soft dough. Using fingers, pat into a 10-inch pie pan. Flute edges. Pierce entire crust with a fork. Bake at 425° for about 12 minutes, or until golden brown. Cool.

Use blender to purée enough berries to make one cup of purée. Reserve rest of fruit in the refrigerator. In a heavy pot, mix together sugar and cornstarch. Add water and strawberry purée. Heat, stirring constantly, until thick and bubbling. Remove from heat. Add lemon juice. Chill completely.

Toss reserved fruit with chilled purée. Pile into cooled pie shell. Serve with a tremendous amount of freshly whipped cream.

Strawberry Cheesecake Topping: Make pie filling as directed and use to top any cheesecake in this book.

Gooey Chocolate Chip and Walnut Pie

This is sort of like pecan pie, only better. It is equally good hot or cold. A generous dollop of freshly whipped cream on top helps cut the richness.

Yield: one 10-inch pie, 8-12 servings

Crust:
- 7 Tablespoons shortening
- 1½ cups all-purpose flour
- ½ teaspoon salt
- 3-5 Tablespoons cold water

Filling:
- 1½ cups butter, melted and cooled
- 3 eggs
- 1 cup sugar
- 1 cup light brown sugar
- 3 Tablespoons flour
- ½ cup semi-sweet chocolate chips
- ½ cup walnuts, coarsely chopped

Preheat oven to 325°. In a medium bowl, cut shortening into flour and salt. Add water, one tablespoon at a time until a dough is formed that sticks together easily. Using fingers, press dough into pie pan. Flute edge. Set aside.

In a large bowl, beat together butter, eggs, sugar, brown sugar and flour until well mixed. Stir in chocolate chips and walnuts. Pour into prepared pie shell. Bake at 325° for 35 minutes or until just set but not firm. Crust should be golden brown. Cool completely before serving.

Cakes, Breads & Other Specialties

Gooey Virginia Peanut Butter Brownies

Make a batch of these to use in my Peanut Butter and Jelly Cheesecake. Since you'll only need about half for the cheesecake, you'll have a few treats to tuck into lunch boxes.

Yield: one 8-inch square pan, 9-12 servings.

1/2	cup butter
1	cup creamy peanut butter
2	cups light brown sugar
1/2	teaspoon salt
1 1/2	teaspoons vanilla
3	eggs
1 1/4	cups all-purpose flour

Preheat oven to 325°. Grease an 8-inch square pan.

Using an electric mixer in a medium bowl, cream together butter, peanut butter, brown sugar, salt and vanilla. Add eggs and flour. Beat on high speed for five minutes. Spread batter into prepared pan. Bake at 325° for about 45 minutes, or until brownies are set and browned. Center will be slightly puffed, but these brownies are gooey and will not test done with a toothpick. Cool in pan for five minutes before removing.

Note: Use the traditional smooth peanut butter that comes in a jar. Freshly ground gourmet peanut butter also works, but it makes a less gooey brownie.

Chocolate Chip Date Cake

The dates almost seem to disappear in this cake, leaving you with the most moist and unusual cake around. It keeps well for days and days. Serve right from the pan with vanilla ice cream.

Yield: one 8-inch square pan, 9-12 servings

1^1/2	cups water
4^3/4	teaspoons baking soda, divided
1	cup chopped, pitted dates
^{3}/4	cup butter
1^1/3	cups sugar, divided
^{1}/4	teaspoon baking powder
^{3}/4	teaspoon salt
2	eggs
1^3/4	cups all-purpose flour
6	ounces semi-sweet chocolate chips

Preheat oven to 350°. Grease an 8-inch square pan.

In a small pot, bring the water to a boil. Add 4½ teaspoons baking soda and dates. Set aside to cool slightly. Meanwhile, in a large bowl, cream together butter, 1 cup sugar, ¼ teaspoon baking soda, baking powder and salt. Add eggs, one at a time, beating well with each addition. Alternately add flour and water-date mixture. Mix well. Pour into prepared pan. Sprinkle chocolate chips over top. Sprinkle ¼ cup sugar over top of chocolate chips. Do not stir.

Bake at 350° for 40-45 minutes or until sides of cake pull away from the sides of the pan. Do not test with toothpick as it will be coated with chocolate and the cake may not appear to be done.

To serve, leave in the pan and cut into squares. Or, cool cake completely, cut into small squares and place each square in a paper muffin cup. Arrange muffin cups on a pretty platter.

Doubley Dark Chocolate Layer Cake

Grandma says this is the thinnest batter she's ever seen. I frost this cake a day in advance and keep it refrigerated, which gives the flavors time to mellow.

Yield: one 8-inch square layer cake, 12-16 servings

Cake batter:
- 1 ³/₄ cups all-purpose flour
- 2 cups sugar
- ³/₄ cup cocoa
- 2 teaspoons baking soda
- 1 teaspoon baking powder
- 1 teaspoon salt
- ¹/₂ cup oil
- 2 eggs
- 1 cup double strength coffee, cooled
- 1 cup buttermilk
- 1 teaspoon vanilla

Frosting:
- 16 ounces powdered sugar
- ³/₄ cup cocoa
- 1 pound butter
- ¹/₂ cup solid white vegetable shortening

Cake: Preheat oven to 350°. Grease two 8-inch square pans. Line with baking parchment or waxed paper. Lightly grease the parchment or waxed paper.

In a large bowl, mix together flour, sugar, cocoa, baking soda, baking powder, and salt. Add oil, eggs, coffee, buttermilk and vanilla. Using an electric mixer, beat until smooth. Divide batter between pans. Bake at 350° for 30 minutes or until cake tests done. Cool in pans before removing cakes.

Frosting: In a medium bowl, sift sugar and cocoa together (important to insure that the frosting is smooth). In a large bowl, using an electric mixer, whip butter and shortening together. Gradually add sifted sugar and cocoa. When combined, whip frosting at high speed until light and fluffy, 3-4 minutes. Frost Doubley Dark Chocolate Layer Cake, using 1 cup frosting between layers and the rest on top and sides. Refrigerate frosted cake until serving time. **Note:** There is no liquid in this frosting.

Coconut & Lemon Cream Cheese Dessert Cake

When I was a Home Economics teacher, this was a favorite treat for staff meetings. The lemon cream cheese is more hunger-satisfying than sweet, so be generous with the pieces.

Yield: one 8-inch square cake, 8-10 servings.

Cake:

6	*Tablespoons butter*
1/2	*teaspoon vanilla*
3/4	*cup sugar*
3	*eggs*
3/4	*cup cake flour*
	grated rind and juice of one lemon

Frosting:

8	*ounces cream cheese, softened*
1	*box (3³/4 ounce) instant lemon pudding mix*
2¹/2	*cups milk, at room temperature*
1	*cup coconut*

Preheat oven to 350°. Grease an 8-inch square pan.

In a large bowl, using an electric mixer, cream together butter, vanilla, and sugar. Add eggs alternately with flour. Beat on high speed for 5 minutes. Stir in juice and rind of lemon. Spread into prepared pan. Bake at 350° for 30 minutes or until done. Cool in pan.

In a large bowl, using an electric mixer, beat cream cheese until fluffy. Gradually add pudding mix and milk. Beat until smooth. Stir in coconut. Pour over top of cooled cake. Refrigerate overnight to blend flavors.

Fresh Blueberry and Sour Cream Scones

These are the plumpest little scones you'll ever find this side of the British Isles, but with our own Virginia twist—ripe blueberries.

Yield: one 10-inch pie pan, 8 scones

> 3   cups all-purpose flour
> 2   Tablespoons baking powder
> 1   teaspoon salt
> 3   Tablespoons sugar
> 1/2 cup butter, softened
> 2   cups sour cream
> 1/4 teaspoon vanilla
> 1/2 cup fresh blueberries

Preheat oven to 350°. Grease a 10-inch pie pan. In a large bowl, using an electric mixer, mix together flour, baking powder, salt, sugar and butter. Add sour cream and vanilla. Mix until smooth. Gently fold in blueberries. Spread batter into pan. Cut through dough in pan, making 8 pie-shaped wedges. Bake at 350° for 30 minutes, until nicely browned. Cool slightly, cut into wedges and serve dusted with powdered sugar.

Fat Free Honey and Whole Wheat Brunch Cake

A delicious, healthy cake that keeps well.

Yield: one 6-cup Turks Head or Bundt cake, 10-16 servings

> 1   cup all-purpose flour
> 2   cups whole wheat flour
> 2   teaspoons baking soda
> 1   cup honey
> 2   cups buttermilk

Preheat oven to 350°. Grease and flour a 6-cup Turks Head or Bundt pan. In a large bowl, using an electric mixer, combine all ingredients. Bake at 350° for 30-35 minutes. Cool in pan about 10 minutes before unmolding. Wrap cooled cake in foil or a large plastic bag and allow to mellow overnight before cutting. Nice dusted with some powdered sugar.

Easy Cheese Strudel

Simple, quick and very impressive. Serve hot or cold.

Yield: one 8-inch square pan, 8-10 servings

- $1^1/2$ pounds cottage cheese
- 3 eggs
- $1^1/4$ teaspoons vanilla
- $3/4$ cup powdered sugar
- 2 Tablespoons cornstarch
- $1/2$ cup butter
- 5 ounces phyllo dough (one third of a 15-ounce package)

Preheat oven to 350°.

In a large bowl, mix together all ingredients except butter and phyllo dough. Set aside. Melt butter in a small sauce pan. Using a pastry brush, brush some of the melted butter on the sides and bottom of an 8-inch square pan. Put a layer of phyllo dough on top of the butter. Brush phyllo with more butter—dough doesn't have to fit neatly into the pan, so just fold it over where needed. Repeat phyllo and butter to make a total of four layers. Top with the cheese mixture. Top with more phyllo and butter layers until all phyllo is used. End with butter.

Bake at 350° for 35-40 minutes or until strudel is puffed up and nicely browned. A toothpick inserted in the center through the phyllo and into the cheese will come up clean when strudel is done.

Cool before cutting. Serve at room temperature or cold. Although best served the same day it is baked, leftover slices that have been refrigerated can be heated in the microwave and served hot. Dust top of strudel generously with powdered sugar before serving.

Karla's Very Fancy Irish Soda Bread

Ask anyone at the Alexandria Farmers' Market about our fragrant soda breads and they will tell you that we never bake enough. We started making these as a lark one St. Patrick's Day some years ago and they were so popular that we haven't stopped.

Yield: one 7-inch round loaf, 8-12 servings.

4½	cups plus 2 teaspoons all-purpose flour
2	teaspoons caraway seed
2¼	teaspoons baking powder
½	teaspoon salt
½	cup sugar
½	cup raisins
¾	cup butter, melted
2	cups hot tap water

Preheat oven to 325°. Grease a 7-inch cheesecake pan.

In a large bowl, mix 4½ cups flour, caraway seed, baking powder, salt, sugar and raisins together. Add butter and continue mixing until the mixture resembles fine crumbs. Add water and mix briefly. Batter should stay lumpy. Spread into pan. Dust with 2 teaspoons flour.

Bake at 325° for 50-60 minutes or until it tests done with a toothpick. Cool 30 minutes before removing from pan.

Fat Free Irish Soda Bread

A variation on our traditional soda bread for people who would like to restrict their sugar and fat intake.

Yield: one 7-inch round loaf, 8-12 servings.

4	cups all-purpose flour
2¹/₂	teaspoons salt
1	teaspoon baking soda
³/₄	teaspoon baking powder
1	cup raisins
1³/₄	cups buttermilk

Preheat oven to 375°. Grease a 7-inch cheesecake pan.

In a large bowl, combine all ingredients except buttermilk. Add the buttermilk all at once and stir briefly until batter is just moistened. Batter should be lumpy. Pour into pan.

Bake at 375° for 40-45 minutes until bread is light brown and sounds hollow when tapped.

Cool in pan five minutes before removing to cooling rack. This bread will not be very brown because there is no sugar in it. Delicious toasted with some orange spiced tea.

Virginia Brown Bread

Moist and dark. Top with sweet butter and jam for tea, or wrap it up and give it as a gift.

Yield: one 9-inch loaf, 8-10 servings.

1½ cups whole wheat flour
¼ cup white flour
½ cup sugar
¼ cup cornmeal
⅔ teaspoon baking soda
¾ teaspoon salt
1 cup milk
1 egg
¼ cup oil
¼ cup molasses

Preheat oven to 325°. Grease a 9"x 5"x 3" loaf pan.

In a large bowl, whisk flours, sugar, cornmeal, baking soda and salt together. Add milk, egg, oil and molasses. Whisk until smooth. Bake at 325° for 45-50 minutes or until done. Cool five minutes in pan before removing. It tastes best when sliced and served the next day.

Double Raisin Chocolate Cinnamon Soda Bread

We eat this lightly toasted with lots of butter and a bit of apricot jam.

Yield: one 7-inch round loaf, 8-12 servings.

4¹/₂	cups plus 2 teaspoons flour
2	teaspoons caraway seed
2¹/₄	teaspoons baking powder
¹/₂	teaspoon salt
1	cup sugar
¹/₃	cup cocoa
³/₄	teaspoon cinnamon
³/₄	cup dark raisins
³/₄	cup butter or margarine, melted
2¹/₄	cups hot tap water

Preheat oven to 325°. Grease a 7-inch cheesecake pan.

In a large bowl, mix together 4½ cups flour, caraway seed, baking powder, salt, sugar, cocoa, cinnamon and raisins. Add butter or margarine and continue mixing until mixture resembles fine crumbs. Add water and mix just to combine. Batter should be lumpy. Spread into pan. Dust with 2 teaspoons of flour.

Bake at 325° for 55-60 minutes or until it tests done with a toothpick. Cool 30 minutes before removing bread from pan.

Pineapple Coconut Upside Down Cake

Not much cake to this one—it is mostly pineapple, coconut and lots of gooey stuff. It is said to be a very old-style American pioneer recipe. When supplies got low, there wasn't always enough sugar to make frosting, but there was usually enough to fancy up a plain cake.

Yield: one 8-inch square cake, 8-10 servings.

$^1/_2$	cup butter, divided
$^3/_4$	cup coconut
1	cup light brown sugar
1	can (20 ounces) crushed pineapple, drained
$^1/_2$	cup sugar
$^1/_4$	teaspoon salt
$^1/_4$	teaspoon baking powder
$^1/_2$	teaspoon vanilla
1	cup plus 2 Tablespoons flour
$^1/_2$	cup buttermilk

Preheat oven to 350°. In an ungreased 8-inch square pan, melt $^1/_4$ cup butter. Rotate pan so butter will cover the bottom and partway up the sides. Over the butter, sprinkle the coconut, then the brown sugar, and then the pineapple. Do not stir. Set aside.

In a large bowl, using an electric mixer, cream together sugar, salt, baking powder, vanilla and remaining $^1/_4$ cup butter. Alternately add the flour and milk. Spread batter over top of brown sugar/pineapple mixture in pan. There is not much batter, so don't worry if the batter doesn't cover completely.

Bake at 350° for 50-60 minutes or until cake is nicely browned and slightly pulls away from the sides of the pan. Cool in pan five minutes, then cut around sides to release cake. Invert onto a serving dish with a rim to catch any drippings. Serve hot or cold with a big scoop of vanilla ice cream.

Hot Chocolate Trifle

This recipe may seem like a trifle—it is only cake and pudding, but it is really nothing to be trifled with. I invented it one Sunday evening when I went to the kitchen looking for some refreshments. There was only some packaged pudding, some leftover cake and a lovely assortment of nice liquids over which one could get quite cordial. The end result is delicious.

Yield: 4 servings

¹/₂	*chocolate cake, baked (page 64)*
1	*package (3³/₄ ounce) dark chocolate pudding mix (not instant)*
¹/₂	*cup espresso or double strength coffee, cooled*
1¹/₂	*cups Half and Half*
¹/₄	*cup Creme de Cocoa*
¹/₄	*cup chocolate syrup*
	whipped cream, for garnish
	cinnamon, for garnish
	chopped peanuts, for garnish

Divide cake between four heat-proof cups. In a heavy saucepan combine pudding mix, espresso, Half and Half, Creme de Cocoa and chocolate syrup. Cook, stirring constantly, over low heat until bubbling all over. Divide hot pudding between cups. Immediately top with piles of whipped cream, a dusting of cinnamon, and a sprinkle of chopped peanuts. Serve immediately.

Sour Cream Coffee Cake

Everyone has a recipe for a sour cream coffee cake buried somewhere in the family treasures. We're including ours just in case you can't find yours.

Yield: one 10-up Bundt pan, 12-16 servings.

3/4	*cup butter*
1 1/2	*cups sugar*
1 1/2	*teaspoons baking powder*
1 1/2	*teaspoons baking soda*
1/2	*teaspoon salt*
2	*teaspoons vanilla*
3	*eggs*
3	*cups flour*
2	*cups sour cream*
3/4	*cup light brown sugar*
1	*Tablespoon cinnamon*
1	*cup coarsely chopped walnuts*

Preheat oven to 350°. Grease a 10-cup Bundt pan.

In a large bowl, cream together butter, sugar, baking powder, baking soda, salt and vanilla using an electric mixer. Add eggs, one at a time, mixing well after each addition. Alternately add flour and sour cream. Mix well. In a separate small bowl, mix together brown sugar, cinnamon and walnuts using a fork or your fingers.

Put 2/3 of batter into a greased Bundt pan. Slightly push batter up the sides and center tube of pan, making a well. Into the well put the brown sugar mixture. Cover the well with remaining batter. Brown sugar mixture doesn't have to be completely covered by batter.

Bake at 350° for 45 minutes or until nicely browned and cake pulls slightly away from the sides of the pan. Cool in pan five minutes and invert onto serving dish. Cool completely before cutting. Sprinkle with powdered sugar.

Apple Brandy Pudding

This is a simple yet elegant dessert for those cold, wintery evenings. It's also a good way to use up leftover cake that's gotten a bit dry. Uncle John likes to have the very last serving of this dessert, because he says it has more flavor and a bit more brandy than the first serving.

Yield: one 8-inch casserole, 12-16 servings.

2	Tablespoons butter
$1/2$	Sour Cream Coffee Cake, baked and coarsely crumbled (page 60)
1	can (21 ounces) apple pie filling
1	cup brandy
1	cup hot water

Preheat oven to 300°. Using entire 2 Tablespoons of butter, grease a casserole that measures 8" round by 3" deep. Into the greased casserole, place alternate layers of cake crumbs and pie filling, beginning and ending with cake crumbs. Pour brandy and water over all. Cover with lid or foil and bake at 300° for at least 90 minutes. The low temperature and slow baking develops the flavor. The exact baking time is not really important. The pudding can be held for several hours by reducing the temperature to 250° and replenishing the liquids as they evaporate. Serve hot with vanilla ice cream or freshly whipped cream.

Note: To serve as part of a buffet, keep warm in a chafing dish, replenishing the liquids as they evaporate. This pudding will perfume the air and set the mood for any winter or holiday party.

A Kiss In The Dark

Dark chocolate cake, bittersweet frosting and a touch of raspberry jam. Where does the name come from? Well, you can feel the raspberry jam but you can't see it... just like any good kiss in the dark.

Yield: one 7-inch torte, 8-12 servings.

Cake Batter:

3/4	cup plus 2 Tablespoons flour
1	cup sugar
6	Tablespoons cocoa
1	teaspoon baking soda
1/2	teaspoon baking powder
1/2	teaspoon salt
1	egg
1/2	cup double strength coffee, brewed and cooled
1/2	cup buttermilk
1/2	teaspoon vanilla
1/4	cup oil

Bittersweet Frosting:

2	cups sour cream, room temperature
3	cups semi-sweet chocolate chips, melted and cooled

Filling: 1/3 cup raspberry jam

Cake: Preheat oven to 350°. Grease a 7-inch cheesecake pan. Line bottom with waxed paper or parchment and grease again. In a large bowl, mix together flour, sugar, cocoa, baking soda, baking powder and salt. Add egg, coffee, buttermilk, vanilla and oil all at once and beat with an electric mixer until smooth. Pour into a prepared pan. Bake at 350 for 40 minutes or until cake tests done. Cool in pan. Invert onto cooling rack and remove paper. Invert again onto serving dish.

Frosting: Whisk sour cream into chocolate a little at a time. The mixture should be satin smooth. Chill if necessary for better spreading consistency.

To assemble: Place cake on serving dish. Trim top if necessary so it is level. Spread top with raspberry jam. Frost entire cake with bittersweet frosting. Smooth frosting with a spatula or a cake comb. Using a pastry bag, pipe remaining frosting on the top (frosting will be thick). Chill to completely set the frosting. Serve in small slices with a dollop of freshly whipped cream along side.

Orange Rye Roll with Orange Whipped Cream

We don't eat many rolled cakes any more. No jelly rolls, no chocolate ice cream logs—I guess folks feel they are too difficult for our modern and fast living times. I hope this recipe changes your mind.

Yield: one 10"x 15" jelly roll pan, 10-12 servings

3	eggs
1	cup sugar
1/4	cup water
2	Tablespoons oil
3/4	teaspoon orange extract
1	cup rye flour
2	teaspoons baking powder
1/4	teaspoon salt
1/4	cup powdered sugar
1	cup heavy cream
1/4	cup sweet orange marmalade

Preheat oven to 375°. Grease a 10" x 15" jelly roll pan. Line bottom with waxed paper. Grease the waxed paper.

In a large bowl, using an electric mixer, beat eggs five minutes. (Don't skimp on the time.) Gradually beat in sugar. Add water, oil and orange extract. Mix briefly. Fold in flour, baking powder and salt. Spread into prepared pan. Bake at 375° for 15-20 minutes until cake tests done. Immediately remove from pan by inverting onto a clean and lint free towel that has been sprinkled with powdered sugar. Remove waxed paper. Immediately roll up towel and cake together (long way or short way). Cool with cake rolled in the towel.

After cake is completely cooled, whip cream and fold in marmalade. Gently unwrap cake and fill with cream mixture (handle cake gently, it will not lay flat). Reroll without the towel and place on a serving dish. Dust with additional powdered sugar.

Variation: Freeze completed cake and serve frozen like an ice cream log.

Plain Good Vanilla Pound Cake

Whenever vanilla pound cake crumbs are called for, I use this recipe.

Yield: one 8-inch square pan, 9-12 servings or 3 cups crumbs

3/4	cup butter or margarine
1 1/2	cups sugar
1	teaspoon vanilla
1 1/2	cups flour
5	eggs

Preheat oven to 350°. Grease an 8-inch square pan. Using an electric mixer, in a large bowl, cream together butter or margarine, sugar and vanilla. Alternately add flour and eggs. After the last addition, beat at high speed for five minutes. Spread into prepared pan and bake at 350° for 40-50 minutes until cake tests done. Cool in pan five minutes before removing.

Plain Good Chocolate Cake

Whenever chocolate cake crumbs are called for, this is the recipe I use.

Yield: one 8-inch square pan, 9-12 servings or 3 cups crumbs

1 1/2	cups flour
6	Tablespoons cocoa
1/4	teaspoon salt
1 1/4	teaspoon baking soda
1 1/2	cups sugar
1 1/2	teaspoons vanilla
1/2	cup oil
1	cup double strength coffee, cooled
1	Tablespoon vinegar

Preheat oven to 350°. Grease an 8-inch square pan. In a large bowl, blend together flour, cocoa, salt, baking soda and sugar. Add vanilla, oil and coffee and mix until smooth. Quickly add vinegar and mix briefly. Mixture will be foamy. Immediately pour into pan and bake at 350° for 40-45 minutes or until toothpick comes out clean. Cool in pan.